# 12 QUESTIONS ABOUT THE
# BILL OF RIGHTS

by Tracey E. Dils

**STORY LIBRARY**

www.12StoryLibrary.com

12-Story Library is an imprint of Peterson Publishing Company and Press Room Editions.

Produced for 12-Story Library by Red Line Editorial

Photographs ©: Stanley Dersh/Library of Congress, cover, 1, 29; Joseph-Siffrède Duplessis/Library of Congress, 4; John Fielding/Library of Congress, 5; Everett Historical/Shutterstock Images, 6, 24, 25, 28; Cvandyke/Shutterstock Images, 7; Constantino Brumidi/Detroit Publishing Co/Library of Congress, 8; Roel Smart/iStockphoto, 9; Pablo Martinez Monsivai/AP Images, 10, 27; wynnter/iStockphoto, 11; Coast-to-Coast/iStockphoto, 12; Richard Thornton/Shutterstock Images, 13; Currier & Ives/Library of Congress, 14; Paul Matthew Photography/Shutterstock Images, 15; North Wind Picture Archives, 16; Dan Howell/Shutterstock Images, 17; bikeriderlondon/Shutterstock Images, 18; a katz/Shutterstock Images, 19; AVN Photo Lab/Shutterstock Images, 20; Robert J. Daveant/Shutterstock Images, 21; trekandshoot/Shutterstock Images, 22; Jacqueline Larma/AP Images, 23; Brandon Bourdages/Shutterstock Images, 26

Content Consultant: Gerard N. Magliocca, JD, Samuel R. Rosen Professor of Law, Indiana University

**Library of Congress Cataloging-in-Publication Data**
Names: Dils, Tracey E., author.
Title: 12 questions about the Bill of Rights / by Tracey E. Dils.
Other titles: Twelve questions about the Bill of Rights
Description: Mankato, MN : 12-Story Library, 2017. | Series: Examining
  primary sources | Includes bibliographical references and index.
Identifiers: LCCN 2016002318 (print) | LCCN 2016002592 (ebook) | ISBN
  9781632352828 (library bound : alk. paper) | ISBN 9781632353320 (pbk. :
  alk. paper) | ISBN 9781621434498 (hosted ebook)
Subjects: LCSH: United States. Constitution. 1st-10th Amendments--Juvenile
  literature. | Civil rights--United States--Juvenile literature.
Classification: LCC KF4749 .D54 2016 (print) | LCC KF4749 (ebook) | DDC
  342.7308/5--dc23
LC record available at http://lccn.loc.gov/2016002318

Printed in the United States of America
Mankato, MN
May, 2016

Access free, up-to-date content on this topic plus a full digital version of this book. Scan the QR code on page 31 or use your school's login at 12StoryLibrary.com.

# Table of Contents

# What Is the Bill of Rights?

The Bill of Rights is a list of additions to the US Constitution. The additions are called amendments. They were added after the Constitution was written.

After the American Revolution, the citizens of the new United States needed to form a government. They wanted it to be different from the British government they had just rebelled against. A group of leaders gathered in 1787 in Philadelphia, Pennsylvania. They included George Washington, Benjamin Franklin, James Madison, and George Mason. Together, they wrote a set of rules and laws. These rules would govern the new land. The rules became the US Constitution.

The Constitution established a strong federal government. But some felt that the Constitution went

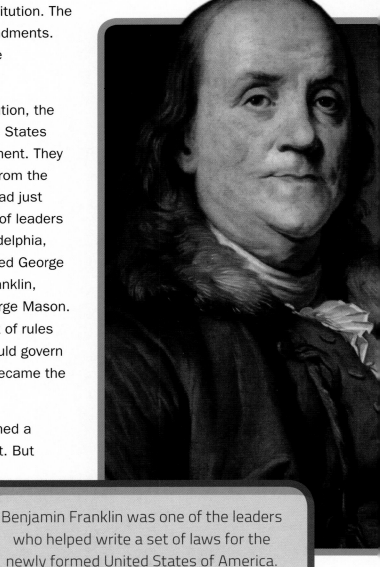

Benjamin Franklin was one of the leaders who helped write a set of laws for the newly formed United States of America.

too far. They feared a strong federal government would limit individual rights. They thought it might also limit the rights of the 13 states. The people had lived under the strong control of England. They wanted to make sure that would not happen again.

That is where the Bill of Rights came in. The amendments in the Bill of Rights ensure personal freedoms. They limit the government's power. They give certain powers to individual states. Without the Bill of Rights, Americans might not enjoy many of the freedoms they have today.

The former colonists wanted to safeguard the rights that were in short supply under England's King George III.

## 10

**Number of amendments in the Bill of Rights.**

- The Bill of Rights is a list of amendments to the US Constitution.
- Americans did not want their federal government to be too strong.
- This document ensures certain freedoms for individuals.
- It also makes clear which powers belong to states and which belong to the federal government.

## GO TO THE SOURCE

To read the full text of the Bill of Rights, go to **www.12StoryLibrary.com/primary**.

# Why Was the Bill of Rights Added to the Constitution?

Some writers of the Constitution believed it was fine as written. This group was led by important men of the time. They included Alexander Hamilton and John Jay of New York and future US president James Madison of Virginia. But a group led by

Virginia delegate George Mason had concerns. They believed the Constitution gave too much power to the government. Madison eventually changed his mind and helped develop the Bill of Rights.

Congress agreed on 12 amendments to the Constitution. The states needed to ratify, or approve, each of them. The states

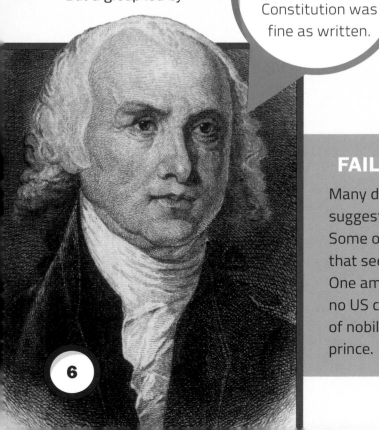

James Madison initially thought the Constitution was fine as written.

## FAILED AMENDMENTS

Many different amendments were suggested for the Bill of Rights. Some of them suggested ideas that seem strange to us today. One amendment proposed that no US citizen should have a title of nobility, such as that of king or prince.

The George Mason Memorial in Washington, DC, commemorates the man credited for making the Bill of Rights possible.

rejected two amendments. One limited the number of representatives in Congress. The other would have kept members of Congress from giving themselves pay raises.

The remaining 10 amendments became the Bill of Rights in 1791. Today, additional amendments have been added to the Constitution. The actual Bill of Rights, however, consists of just the first 10 amendments.

## 19
### Number of amendments Madison originally proposed.

- Some writers of the Constitution did not want the Bill of Rights added.
- Two amendments were rejected by the states and did not make it to the Bill of Rights.
- The Bill of Rights was added to the Constitution in 1791.

# Who Wrote the Bill of Rights?

Most experts believe that James Madison was the main author of the Bill of Rights. He likely drew upon the ideas of George Mason. Mason had written the Virginia Declaration of Rights in 1776. This document stated that all Virginians had specific rights. Both Mason and Madison were from Virginia.

Mason had strong ideas about the rights of individuals. Madison was influenced by fellow Virginian and future president Thomas Jefferson.

## 1
**Number of founders most often credited with writing the Bill of Rights.**

- James Madison is regarded as the author of the Bill of Rights.
- The Bill of Rights was modeled after the Virginia Declaration of Rights.
- Madison was influenced by Thomas Jefferson and George Mason.

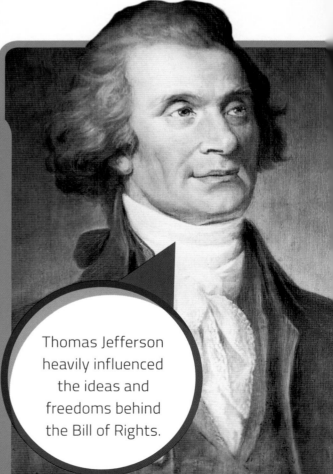

Thomas Jefferson heavily influenced the ideas and freedoms behind the Bill of Rights.

# Magna Carta of King John, AD 1215

A replica of the Magna Carta

At the time, Jefferson was an ambassador in France. He had hoped that the Constitution would include a bill of rights. He proposed the idea of a bill of rights in a letter to Madison.

## BRITISH ROOTS

The Constitution was influenced by a document called the Magna Carta (or Great Charter). This document was an attempt to outline certain individual rights in England in 1215. Many of those same ideas were included in the Bill of Rights.

# 4

# How Does the Bill of Rights Promote Individual Rights?

The Constitution is a powerful document. But it does not specifically mention certain individual rights. It also does not make clear which rights belong to the states. The Bill of Rights describes the freedoms that belong to all Americans. It is based on the idea that all human beings have certain rights that cannot be taken away. It details the areas in which states cannot overrule the federal government.

For example, the government cannot forbid a newspaper or news channel to speak out against it. The Bill of Rights guarantees freedom of the press. The government also cannot establish an official religion

The Bill of Rights guarantees the media the right to report on the government without interference.

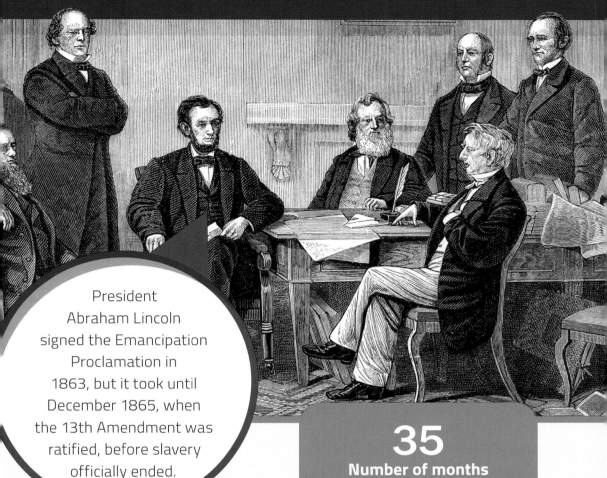

President Abraham Lincoln signed the Emancipation Proclamation in 1863, but it took until December 1865, when the 13th Amendment was ratified, before slavery officially ended.

that its citizens must follow. The Bill of Rights ensures freedom of religion for all American citizens.

However, neither the Bill of Rights nor the Constitution originally applied to all Americans. For example, slaves were still considered property. They did not become official US citizens until the 14th Amendment was ratified on July 9, 1868.

## 35

**Number of months between the issuing of the Emancipation Proclamation and the ratification of the 13th Amendment.**

- The Bill of Rights states the freedoms that individuals have.
- It also outlines which rights belong to the states.
- Slaves were not considered citizens at the time the Bill of Rights was written.

# What Rights Does the First Amendment Grant?

The First Amendment in the Bill of Rights guarantees many important rights. These rights all cover different ways people express themselves. One is freedom of speech. That means citizens have the right to state their opinions. Americans can say what they want without fear of the government trying to silence them.

The First Amendment also grants freedom of religion. It allows all Americans to practice whatever faith they choose. They can also practice no religion at all. It also protects religious groups from government interference.

The freedom to assemble is one of the key rights granted by the First Amendment.

**1991**
Year the First Amendment Center was created to educate Americans about the amendment.

- The First Amendment establishes many important rights.
- It guarantees freedom of speech and religion.
- It also guarantees freedom of the press.

Religious freedom is another right that the First Amendment guarantees American citizens.

were under British rule, these freedoms were often limited. That's why the new leaders felt so strongly about them.

The First Amendment protects the freedom of the press. It allows the media to report news without fear of the government. Journalists can speak out against government officials.

The First Amendment also gives citizens the right to assemble. That means they can gather to work for a cause or concern. In addition, it protects the rights of citizens to call on the government to deal with a particular issue. When the colonies

## THINK ABOUT IT

The First Amendment outlines a number of important rights that deal with how we express ourselves. Which of them do you think is the most important? Support your opinion with facts.

# Why Was the Second Amendment Created?

The Second Amendment gives people the right to bear arms. That means citizens are allowed to own guns. The amendment states that a "well-regulated militia" is important to any free state. A militia is a small army of private citizens.

When the Bill of Rights was written, the United States had just broken free from Great Britain. Under British rule, the colonists could not legally use guns to defend themselves. The leaders of the new country believed in the right to bear arms. They wanted to have guns to defend themselves and their families.

A colonial militia, led by a drummer and a fifer, march off to war.

# WE HAVE GUNS

Gun control is one of the most controversial issues in the United States today.

The Second Amendment is a major topic of debate today. Many people argue that the idea of a militia is outdated. They say the founders could not have imagined the types of weapons available to the public today. The amendment's supporters argue that many restrictions on gun rights are unconstitutional. The debate is controversial and often a major topic in political discussions.

## 310 million

**Approximate number of guns owned by US citizens.**

- The right to bear arms is guaranteed in the Second Amendment.
- The right to own guns was important to colonists, who were unable to do so under British rule.
- Today, the country still debates whether people should be able to own guns or what types of guns should be available.

15

# Why Was the Third Amendment Important?

Can you imagine having to let enemy soldiers live in your home? That's exactly what happened before and during the American Revolution. The Quartering Act of 1774 said that colonists had to welcome British soldiers into their homes. They were also expected to feed the soldiers and take on other expenses. This angered the colonists. Many considered the British soldiers

## 3

**Number of major wars fought on American soil.**

- The Quartering Act of 1774 allowed British soldiers to live in colonists' homes.
- This issue was a key cause of the American Revolution.
- The Third Amendment says US citizens do not have to let soldiers live in their homes.
- The Third Amendment does not get much attention today because so few wars have been fought on US soil.

Colonists could not stop British troops from entering—or even living in—their homes.

enemies. The issue fueled the rebellion.

Citizens of the new United States did not want this to be allowed in their country. The Third Amendment protects homeowners from being forced to let soldiers live in their homes. The amendment may seem strange to us today. But in the early days of the United States, it was very important.

The American Revolution was one of the few wars fought on what is now US soil. For this reason, the amendment really has not affected our lives today. Even so, it helps to protect the property and privacy rights of US citizens.

Some people consider the attacks on New York City and Washington, DC, on September 11, 2001, an act of war on US soil.

## WARS IN AMERICA

Only three wars have been fought on US soil. Besides the American Revolution, only the War of 1812 and the US Civil War were waged within our borders. However, the United States was drawn into World War II by the attack on Pearl Harbor, Hawaii. And the terrorist attacks on New York City and Washington, DC, on September 11, 2001, have been considered an act of war by some.

# What Do Amendments Four through Seven Cover?

The next four amendments primarily deal with the rights of people who are accused of crimes. In colonial times, the rights of the citizens were not clearly defined. Officials could enter a citizen's home to search it without the owner's permission. People who committed even small crimes could be punished severely. The Fourth, Fifth, Sixth, and Seventh Amendments

sought to change that. Together they promise a system that will fairly judge those accused of a crime.

The Fourth Amendment says that law enforcement officials need a search warrant based on probable cause in order to search people or their property. This means a judge has to decide that the police have a good reason to conduct a search. One of the important freedoms guaranteed by the

US citizens are guaranteed a trial in front of a jury of their peers.

Police need a search warrant to enter a home without the owner's permission.

## WHAT DO YOU THINK?

A jury is made up of the accused's "peers." That means the jury members are regular citizens, not legal experts. Do you think that is wise? Or do you think juries should be made up of people who have a background in the law?

# 12

**Number of jury members that are usually assigned to a criminal trial.**

- The Fourth, Fifth, Sixth, and Seventh Amendments mostly deal with the rights of people accused of crimes.
- Under British rule, many of the citizens' rights were unclear.
- These amendments help guarantee that people accused of crimes are treated fairly.

Fifth Amendment is the right to avoid self-incrimination. That means you don't have to testify if you are on trial. The Sixth Amendment says that jury trials cannot be unnecessarily delayed. They also must be held in public. It also says that a person accused of a crime must be told what the charges are. Finally, the Seventh Amendment sets the rules for a jury trial in cases that do not involve crimes.

# What Does the Eighth Amendment Say about Punishment?

The Eighth Amendment ensures that fines or bail are reasonable. Bail is an amount of money paid to the court to release a prisoner. It is one way to make sure that the person accused of a crime will appear in court. People lose their bail money if they don't return for their trial. The bail amount is determined by the severity of the crime the suspect is accused of committing. This portion of the amendment has faced scrutiny as the average size of bail payments has increased significantly over the years.

The Eighth Amendment dictates that bail must be reasonable.

STOP EXECUTIONS!

MARIANIST SOC.JUSTICE COLLABORATIVE

The amendment also states that punishment may not be cruel or unusual. At the time the Bill of Rights was written, many punishments were exactly that. A person could be hanged for a simple crime like burglary. Other harsh forms of punishment were also common.

Today in the United States, these punishments have changed. But many states still issue death sentences for the most serious

Opponents of the death penalty say it defies the Eighth Amendment's ban of "cruel and unusual" punishment.

crimes. Each state determines whether it will use the death penalty. Most executions are by lethal injection. That method is supposed to make death less painful, and thus, less cruel than other methods. However, some human rights advocates believe that any form of the death penalty is cruel and unusual. In their opinion, the Eighth Amendment forbids it.

21

# 10

# What Do Amendments Nine and Ten Concern?

The Ninth and Tenth Amendments limit the power of the federal government. These amendments do not list specific powers, however. They say that the list of powers outlined in the document is not final. The amendments were added to keep the federal government from claiming all powers not specifically mentioned.

The Ninth Amendment says that freedoms not clear in the Constitution belong to the people. This amendment is not used very often. But it has been used to support protecting individual privacy.

The Tenth Amendment says that the federal government has only the powers granted by the Constitution. Any additional freedoms are up to individual states. This amendment has been used to limit

The federal government's powers are more clearly defined by the Ninth and Tenth Amendments.

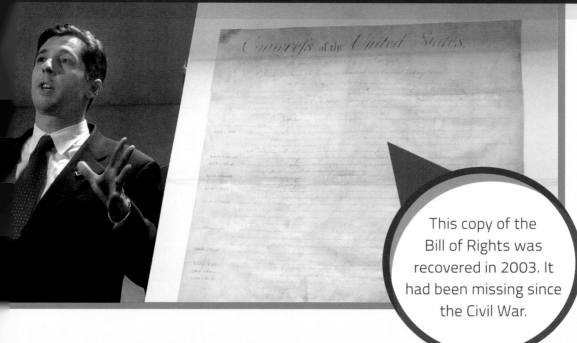

This copy of the Bill of Rights was recovered in 2003. It had been missing since the Civil War.

the power of the federal government. It has also been used to regulate business, trade, and taxation.

## WHO STOLE THE BILL OF RIGHTS?

Before the Bill of Rights was enacted, George Washington arranged for 14 handwritten copies of it to be made. One copy went to each of the 13 states. The other went to the US Congress. During the Civil War, North Carolina's copy disappeared. In 2003, an undercover agent seized it from a collector. It was returned to the North Carolina State Capitol.

# 0

**Number of rights or powers that the Ninth and Tenth Amendments give the federal government.**

- The last two amendments in the Bill of Rights do not deal with specific freedoms.
- These amendments say that the government's powers are stated in the Constitution.
- All powers not mentioned in the Constitution belong to individual states.

# Are There Any Other Amendments to the Constitution?

The Bill of Rights comprised just the first 10 amendments to the US Constitution. The Constitution is known as a "living document." That means it can change. Currently, the Constitution has 27 amendments. To amend the Constitution, two-thirds of the US House of Representatives has to approve. Then, two-thirds of the US Senate must approve the amendment. Finally, three-fourths of the states have to approve

The 21st Amendment repealed, or overturned, the 18th Amendment.

## 17

**Number of amendments that have been added since the Bill of Rights was adopted.**

- The 18th Amendment made it illegal to make, sell, or transport alcohol for 13 years before it was repealed.
- The 13th Amendment made slavery illegal in 1865.
- Women were not given the right to vote until 1920, when the 19th Amendment was passed.

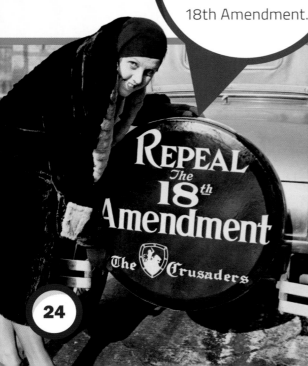

for the amendment to be added to the Constitution.

Sometimes an amendment can cancel out a previous amendment. For example, the 18th Amendment made it illegal to make, sell, or transport alcohol. That lasted until 1933. Then, the 21st Amendment was passed. It made drinking alcohol legal again.

Other amendments gave important civil rights to citizens who had been discriminated against. After the Civil War, in 1865, Congress passed the 13th Amendment. It made slavery illegal. President Abraham Lincoln had issued the Emancipation Proclamation in 1863. But that was not a law. Lincoln died before the 13th Amendment was ratified.

The 19th Amendment gave women the right to vote in 1920. Before that time, many people thought women should not have a role in the political process. Tireless advocates made women's suffrage happen.

## SUSAN B. ANTHONY

The 19th Amendment is often called the Susan B. Anthony Amendment. Anthony was born in 1820. She worked for women's suffrage, or the right to vote. Anthony became interested in suffrage when she was not permitted to speak at a meeting because she was a woman. She died in 1906. The amendment that allowed women to vote was not passed until 1920. Though she did not live to see it, Anthony set the stage for women's suffrage.

# Who Makes Sure that the Amendments Are Followed?

The courts of the United States justice system help to make sure the amendments are being followed. The US Supreme Court is often asked to rule on cases involving how the Constitution is interpreted. The members of the Supreme Court are called justices. They are experts in law and the Constitution. Unless they choose to resign or retire, the justices serve for the rest of

their lives. There are nine justices on the Supreme Court.

A case comes to the Supreme Court after it is reviewed by local courts. The justices review the case and decide whether or not they will accept it. If they do, both sides argue their case. Then, the justices form their opinions. The majority opinion reflects the court's final decision. One justice who is in

The US Supreme Court Building

The Supreme Court consists of nine justices who receive lifetime appointments to the bench.

the majority writes an essay that justifies the decision. Judges who disagree can write a dissenting opinion that disagrees with the majority opinion. That way, all opinions are recorded for future review.

The Supreme Court bases its decisions on the Constitution. The 10 amendments that make up the Bill of Rights are frequently cited in its rulings.

# 6

**Original number of justices on the Supreme Court when the Bill of Rights was added to the Constitution.**

- The justices of the Supreme Court are the protectors of the Constitution, making sure laws do not violate it.
- The majority and minority opinions are preserved for the record.
- Once they are appointed, Supreme Court justices can serve for the rest of their lives.

# Fact Sheet

- Freedom of speech in the First Amendment doesn't just apply to speech; it applies to actions as well. In 1984, one man burned the American flag as a protest. He was arrested. The Supreme Court later ruled that his action was supported by freedom of speech.

- Women's fight for the right to vote lasted 100 years, until the 19th Amendment was passed. An amendment was proposed in 1923 to guarantee the rights of women. This amendment, called the Equal Rights Amendment, was approved by Congress in 1972, but the states did not ratify it.

- The Bill of Rights has legal force in the United States. That means that any act of Congress that goes against the Bill of Rights will likely be brought before the Supreme Court.

- The first black member of the Supreme Court was Thurgood Marshall, who began serving in 1967. Sandra Day O'Connor became the first woman to serve on the Supreme Court in 1981.

- Prohibition, established by the 18th Amendment, was not supported by many doctors. That's because many of the medicines they gave to patients had alcohol as an ingredient. Those who fought for prohibition were called "drys." Those who did not want prohibition were called "wets."

- The term "Bill of Rights" is widely used to describe documents that protect special groups of people. For instance, Ohio has a Nursing Home Patient Bill of Rights. It states the rights that are guaranteed to those who are living in a nursing home.

# Glossary

**ambassador**
A person who represents his or her country in another country.

**bail**
Money given to release a prisoner until the prisoner faces trial.

**burglary**
Breaking into a building to steal something.

**delegate**
Someone who represents an organization or a cause.

**dissenting**
Disagreeing.

**jury trial**
A legal proceeding in which a group of people listens to evidence and makes a decision.

**militia**
A group of people with some military training called to action during emergencies.

**Prohibition**
A period of time in American history when alcohol was illegal.

**ratify**
To vote to approve.

**statesman**
A politician, diplomat, or other public figure who works in a governmental capacity.

**suffrage**
The right to vote.

**testify**
To state the truth or give evidence in a court of law.

# For More Information

## Books

Leavitt, Amie Jane. *The Bill of Rights*. Hockessin, DE: Mitchell Lane, 2012.

Swain, Gwenyth. *Documents of Freedom: A Look at the Declaration of Independence, the Bill of Rights, and the US Constitution*. Minneapolis, MN: Lerner Publications, 2012.

Wolfe, James and Nancy L. Stair. *Understanding the Bill of Rights*. New York: Enslow Publishing, 2016.

## Visit 12StoryLibrary.com

Scan the code or use your school's login at **12StoryLibrary.com** for recent updates about this topic and a full digital version of this book. Enjoy free access to:

- Digital ebook
- Breaking news updates
- Live content feeds
- Videos, interactive maps, and graphics
- Additional web resources

**Note to educators:** Visit 12StoryLibrary.com/register to sign up for free premium website access. Enjoy live content plus a full digital version of every 12-Story Library book you own for every student at your school.

# Index

## About the Author

Tracey E. Dils is the author of more than 40 books for young readers. She has been awarded the Ohioana Award in Children's Literature. Tracey graduated from the College of Wooster in Wooster, Ohio, and lives with her husband in Columbus, Ohio.

## READ MORE FROM 12-STORY LIBRARY

Every 12-Story Library book is available in many formats. For more information, visit 12StoryLibrary.com.